TRANSACTIONAL ANALYSIS FOR EVERYBODY SERIES

TA for KIDS

(...and grown-ups too.....)

by
Alvyn M. Freed Ph.D.

Published by JALMAR PRESS INC.

Distributed by Price/Stern/Sloan Publishers, Inc.
Los Angeles, California 90048

1st Printing, 1971 — 1,000 books
2nd Printing, 1971 — 2,000 books
3rd Printing, 1972 — 10,000 books
4th Printing, 1973 — 20,000 books
5th Printing, 1974 — 50,000 books

TABLE OF CONTENTS

TABLE OF ILLUSTRATIONS

Illustrations by Joann Dick

ACKNOWLEDGEMENTS

I wish to extend my appreciation to:

Dr. Thomas Harris, M.D., who introduced me to TA in 1966. His encouragement to use TA in the private practice of psychology led to the present book.

To the members of my groups, especially the boys and girls in the Friday meetings who have patiently and (sometimes) enthusiastically listened to and encouraged me to continue with "the book."

To my colleagues Ned and Carol Budlong whose thinking and caring are an integral part of the text and whose enthusiastic encouragement provided a needed impetus.

To Sue Baker, my wonderful secretary, whose patience through many rewrites is unending (thus far).

To my wife, Marge, my sons, Larry and Mark, and my mother, Mrs. Amy Freed, who make my life and work worth the effort.

To all of you — You're OK.

Alvyn M. Freed, Ph D.

INTRODUCTION

"TA for Kids" is the first of a series to present Transactional Analysis (TA) to boys and girls (and their important grown-ups) in short words and simple phrases. Simplicity makes it easier to use TA concepts everyday. I think children will find this useful. The text draws on Dr. Eric Berne's "TA in Psychoanalysis," his best selling "Games People Play" and Dr. Tom Harris' "I'm OK — You're OK" as well as on my experience in presenting these ideas to the members of my groups. The series, geared to different age and grade levels, will enable pupils, their mothers and fathers and their teachers to make sense to each other.

"TA for Kids" was intended to be used by boys and girls in grades III-VI, but others of all ages find that its clarity enhances their interest in TA. Efforts are made to stroke the Kid and feed the Adult. The book is written in such a way that it may be read *by* boys and girls or *to* them by grown-ups. In my groups the children enjoyed listening. Sometimes they would take turns reading aloud to each other. The tests and exercises at the close of the chapters have excited and delighted the youngsters and encouraged them to continue learning.

When the book was used with groups of children in the seven to eleven range the effects were as I hoped. In each session the children enjoyed listening to the chapter and participating in the post-chapter tests. Individual failure is minimized and success guaranteed. Failures are avoided since the children can refer to each other to get correct answers. A knowledge of TA concepts is thus acquired and is retained for long periods of time. One unexpected outcome in using the book is the amount of discussion it generates among the children and the ease with which the children are turned on. A second was the unexpected delight which grown-ups derive in increased understanding of TA.

For teachers the book is a handy manual. Each chapter can be used in a 45 minute session. This leaves about 15 minutes for refreshments and social transactions among the children. Frequently during the refreshment period discussion of the text continues and other examples of how kids acquire strokes are discovered.

The first book, "TA for Kids" is part of a series called "TA for Everybody." It will be followed by texts designed for other age groups. "TA for Kids" can be used in psychology classes, mental health groups, PTA Study groups, TA groups or at home.

CHAPTER I — WHO ARE YOU?

You are three people. You thought you were just one. No, you're really three. Oh, not a person with three heads, nor are there three little people running around inside you. But, inside of each of us, you and me, there are three different people. These three people make you and me do what we do and each of them is different. They're as different as you and I are different. For you and me to understand ourselves, to know why we do what we do, we have to get acquainted. We have to know these three people pretty well. I have nicknamed the three people inside me MEP, MEA, and MEC (see Figure 1). These three nicknames stand for the three ME's. There is the Parent Me, the Adult Me and the Child Me. Now you didn't know you had a Parent inside you, but you do. You also have a part of you which we call the Adult. This is the grown-up, which knows how to make decisions. And there is the part of you we call the Child. I guess you know about him. He occupies a great deal of your time and makes many of your right now decisions. Right?

The Parent is very much like Father and Mother. I call the Parent inside me MEP. The MEP in me is a *very bossy* (Figure 2) but a very kind person. He tells me and others what to do. If I don't follow his orders, I sometimes feel afraid or guilty. That feeling of being afraid or guilty is ME Child or MEC. But MEP loves to do things for other people. He says, "Here is a nice piece of cake and a glass of milk for you, Hon," when my son comes home. Sometimes my wife says, "I'll get it, you sit still." That's her MEP taking care of me. Do you have the kind of MEP in you that likes to take care of and do things for other people?

1

THE THREE ME'S

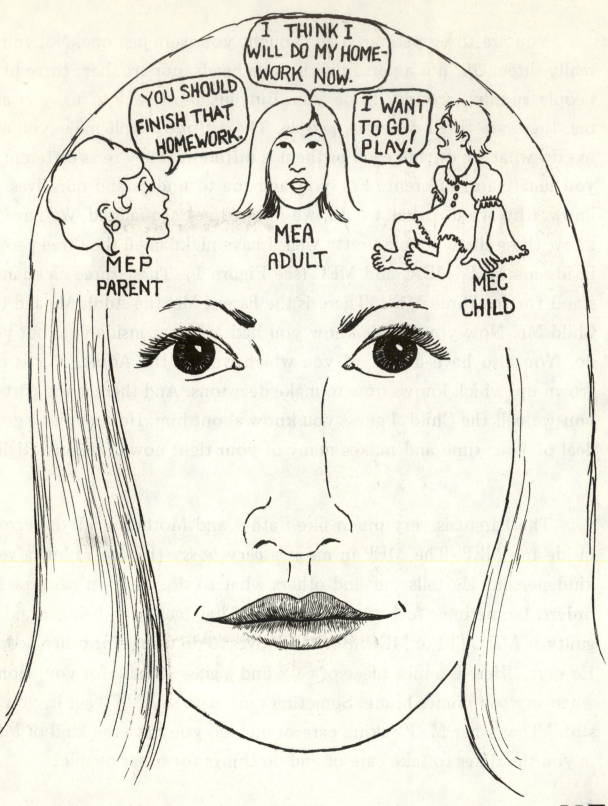

YOU ARE REALLY THREE PEOPLE

2

MEP
MEA
MEC fig

fig. 2

The MEC (or the Child-in-me) is the part of me that is very much like I was when I was a little boy. I had feelings and ways of acting like a little boy because I *was* little. You know, when I was little I would talk to my dog. And I'd run after him and he'd chase me as I scrambled on all fours. Mother would say, "Oh, you're being a doggie." I used to like to swim in a little creek that ran near our house and I loved to eat. Do you like to do those things?

I liked to have fun when I was little and I still do. That part of me which likes fun is the Child-in-me. I call that part MEC or ME-Child. Inside my Child along with good feelings there are some angry or hurt feelings. Sometimes my Child is sad and unhappy. Often I did things that got me into trouble (Figure 3). Has that ever happened to you? Do you ever feel sad or hurt or angry? I still do. Are you sad? (Talk about that right now to whoever is with you.)

The third Me is what I call the Adult or MEA. He is the fellow inside me that figures things out. If he can get the facts he can look at them and make sense. He can study and learn. We'll talk a lot about him later, but right now just remember that MEA is the one who makes sense, who learns and can make decisions, who keeps the other two out of trouble if he is strong and healthy.

MEC HOOKED

fig.3

Now we've learned that there are three people inside of us. We call these people MEP, MEA and MEC or Parent, Adult and Child. They're the people who cause us to behave the way we do. To know each "ME" will help you to know other people. To know our three ME's helps us to know ourselves and to know other people. That's happiness. Now here is a list of words. 1) See how many of them you use and how many your folks use. 2) See if you can locate your Parent, Adult and Child when you use them. 3) Later see if you can detect Mother's Parent, Adult and Child when she speaks. Or Daddy's or your friend's. But don't tell them. Keep it a secret.

Here are the words, label each of them with a P, A or C, short for MEP, MEA or MEC:

× 1. ouch _A_

2. darn it _c_

3. you're bad _P_

4. bed time, dear _P_

× 5. I'd rather _c_

6. I see _A_

7. it's getting late _A_

8. you're too noisy _P_

9. I wish _c_

10. you're filthy _P_

11. eat, eat it's good for you _P_

12. I don't want to go to bed _c_

× 13. I laugh happily _A_

× 14. I feel good _A_

15. you're just a trouble maker _P_

× 16. shut up _P_

17. don't be childish _P_

18. I don't care _C_

19. I'm afraid of the dark _c_

20. Oh! I want to eat and eat all the ice cream I can get _C_

(To find out if you labeled them correctly turn to page 80 and you'll see the answers.)

7

CHAPTER II — ME THE PARENT (MEP)

In the last chapter we talked about three people inside of us. We called him the Parent, the Adult and the Child. We gave them nicknames: MEP, MEA and MEC which stand for Me the Parent, Me the Adult and Me the Child. Now, today we are going to talk just about Me the Parent or MEP. When we were little we needed Mother and Daddy to teach us what to do (Figure 4) and we learned a great many things from them that they never taught us. They taught us how to be mothers and fathers, men and women, husband and wife by doing the things they did. When we saw them talk to each other, we learned that that's what husbands and wives do. You may remember when you were very little, sometimes you played with dolls and you spanked the doll. Who did you learn that from? Or you played house and you wanted to use Mother's clothes and dress up and act like a big lady. Now that I've grown up I sometimes act the way my father acted. That's my Parent. When you were acting like Mother that was your Parent. Each mother and father usually acts the way their mother and daddy acted. When you see and hear yourself acting like your mother or father would act or would have you act, that's MEP speaking.

The Parent is a good part of us. The Parent tells MEC what to do when MEC is puzzled. Sometimes you've heard Daddy say things like, "Children should be seen and not heard," or when he gives us a spanking he says, "This hurts me more than it does you." Which part of Daddy is talking? Right. His Parent! Why? Because that's what his father said to him. When you hear yourself saying to someone else,

WE NEED MOTHERS

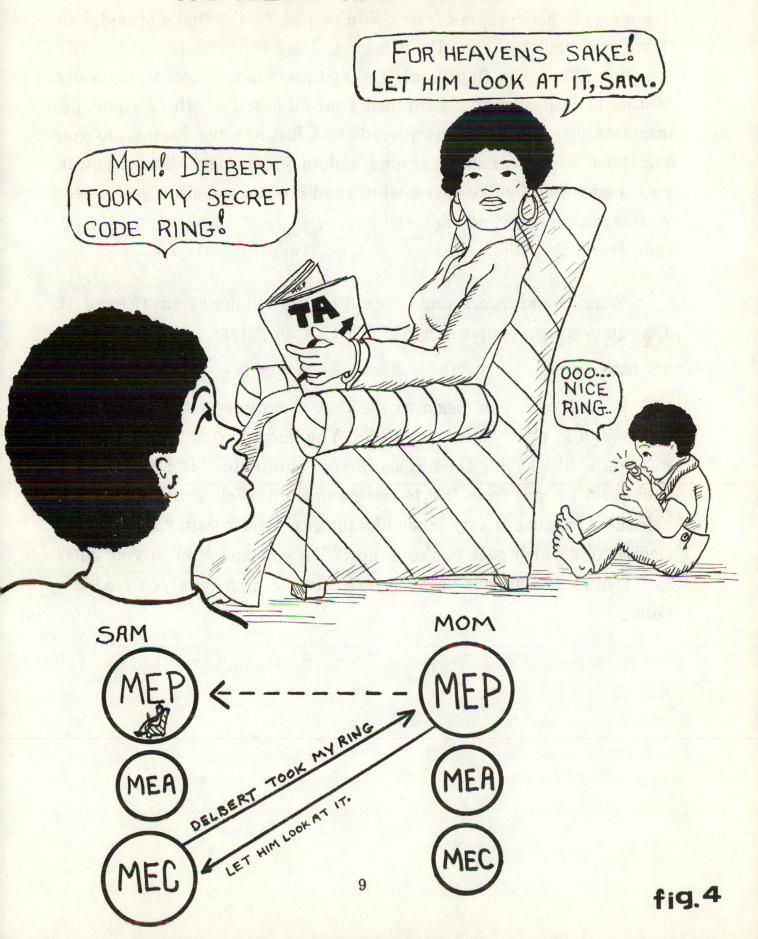

fig.4

"Don't talk back to me," or "You're bad," or "That's stupid," or "You're ridiculous," or "Do it because I say so." (Figure 5) it's MEP speaking. When you find yourself using those kinds of words, it's really Mother or Daddy speaking through your mouth. The other two people inside of you have their own words too, just like the Parent. Do you ever boss brother or sister around and they get angry? That's you in your Parent (acting like "guess who") and brother and sister get bossed. Who is getting angry? (Child! Right.)

When Grandma is fixing your cut leg she's in her Parent (Figure 6). Do you ever help people like that? That's your Parent.

I think you can begin to see that sometimes your Parent is in charge and at other times your Child. You know having three people to run you is like having three gears in your automobile. Did you ever see Daddy shift gears, from first to second to third? Well, shifting from one person to another is very much like the gear shift in your car. Have you figured out which gear you're in now? Do you know when you shift? See if you can find out between now and the next time you read this book.

PECKING ORDER

fig.5

PARENT AT WORK

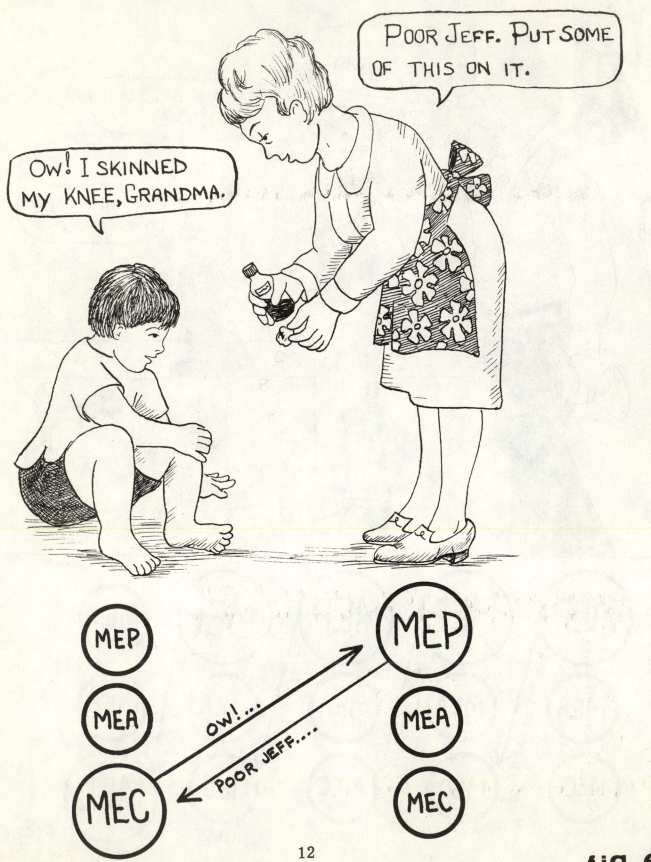

fig. 6

SHIFTING GEARS

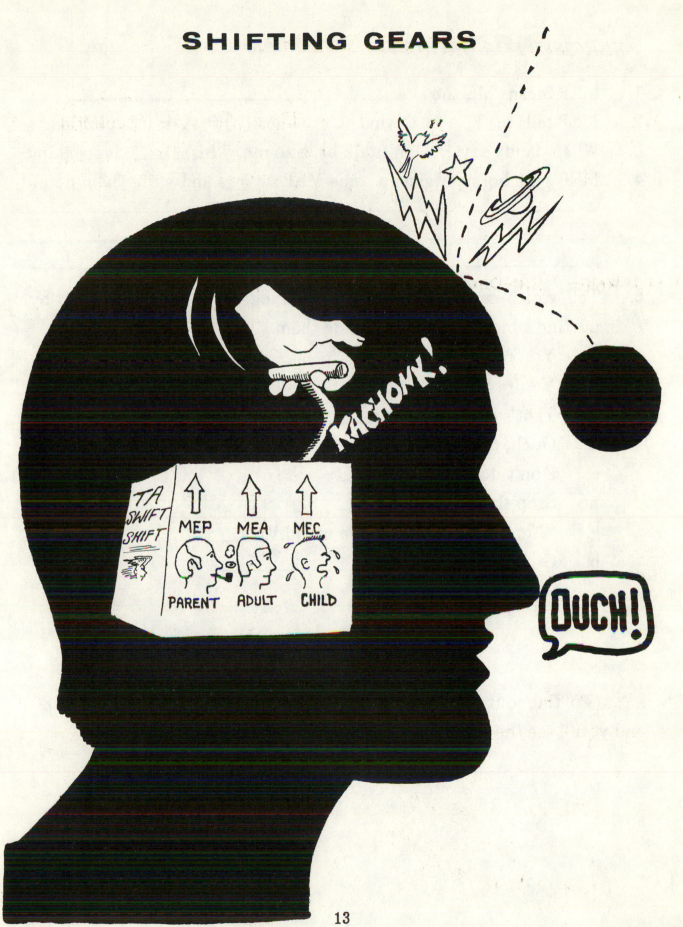

fig. 6a

EXERCISES FOR GROUP

1. MEP means ME the _Parent_

2. MEP tells (a) P, A or Ⓒ what to do when (b) P, A or Ⓒ is puzzled.

3. When daddy says, "Don't talk back to me, " his _P_ is speaking.

4. MEP's are bossy. Make up some MEP sayings and write them here.

    _____

    _____

    _____

5. Tell which of the following are talking: MEA, MEP or MEC by putting a big P, A or C alongside them.

    a. You're being silly. _P_

    b. You're lazy. _P_

    c. That's correct. _A_

    d. Ouch, that hurt. _C_

    orC e. Don't do that. _P_

    f. Stop that noise. _P_

    g. "I'm sitting on top of the world." _C_

    h. Go to bed this minute. _P_

(To find out if you have labeled them correctly turn to page 80 and you'll see the answers.)

CHAPTER III — ME THE CHILD (MEC)

When I first used the word *child* in this book you knew it to mean little boy or girl. Now we're using it to mean the part of us which "feels." Do you hear a noise? Feel a breeze? Smell something? If you say "yes," it's your ME Child speaking. Do you ever get scared? Laugh? Like to swim? Get angry? (Figure 7) These are all things your Child does. The Child spelled with a Capital "C" is one of our best parts. We take pretty good care of it most of the time. But sometimes we let it do what it wants, like eat sour apples (get sick) or stay up too late (get tired) or get hurt (be sad). In these cases we're not letting MEA or MEP protect MEC (or themselves) and the Child gets sick or in trouble.

Sometimes you'll say words or make sounds like a little baby or an animal just for fun. Make some now: cat, dog, pig, etc. That's your Child. Sometimes you'll make believe you're a king, an airplane, a great fighter or an astronaut. (That's your Child using imagination.) Grown-ups sometimes call it daydreaming. You know if it wasn't for daydreaming there'd never be any inventions.

Fun is a Child at work. Your Child is the most important part of you. MEA and MEP have the job of protecting MEC, for old Brainless can't think — he just has fun. The trouble is that sometimes MEC wants more fun than MEP, MEA or anyone else can take and so MEP and MEA have to protect themselves as well as everybody else. MEP may

THE CHILD AT WORK

LOVE

PLAY

PAIN

FEAR

fig.7

punish or MEA say "No." When that happens MEC may get angry and sulk. Do you ever sulk? I do. Not much fun, is it? But what else is there to do when you can't have what you want, you don't think it's fair and you aren't "allowed" to talk about it.

Sometimes when Child gets too angry or "strong" it messes up Adult and shuts off Parent (Figure 8). The part I've marked with an "X" is where the Child has "messed up" (contaminated) Adult and MEA can't think. Do you ever shut off your Parent tapes and mess up MEA? It's fun while it lasts but Oh, boy! when it's over! "Why did you do that?" asks Mother's MEA or MEP. Your MEA can't answer, your Parent can't answer and old Brainless can only say (all together) "I DON'T KNOW." That doesn't go over very big, does it?

That's two, now. Parent and Child. Today we learned where we have fun and how sometimes when we let the "Kid" run wild, without a "brain" to guide him, he can get us into trouble. Willful Willy, the Child, can "mess up" MEA. We called that "con-tam-i-nation." Try to remember that word. OK?

ANGRY CHILD

fig.

EXERCISES FOR GROUP

Did your Adult get this?

1. Only the Child has feelings. (True) or false.

2. When the Child takes over it ___messes___ up the Adult.

3. Messing up the Adult by MEC is called _con fam ip nation_ !

4. The Child doesn't think. (True) or false.

5. The Child feels. (True) or false.

6. The Child is where we have fun. (True) or false.

7. MEC is the one we call "Ol' Brainless." (True) or false.

8. Fun is the ___Child___ at work.

(To find out if you have labeled them correctly turn to page 80 and you'll see the answers.)

CHAPTER IV — ME THE ADULT (MEA)

Well, if MEP is a tape recording of your Mother and Dad and MEC is "old Brainless — have fun," what do you think with? You've guessed it — ME Adult or MEA. MEA is the one who figures things out. MEA gets the facts and looks at them. And when MEA speaks, he makes sense. MEA works like a cash register (Figure 9). You know you've seen the cash register at the grocery store. The man pushes buttons, one push for each thing mother buys. Then he pushes another button, wheels whir and then, zoom! out comes the total amount she owes and the right change. MEA's like that — puts in facts, jiggles them around and pops out the answer but a million times faster than any machine. A machine which handles facts this way is called a computer (cahm-pew-ter).

Your brain is a bigger and better computer than any machine that was ever built by man (Figure 10). You know, I read where a big company had built a computer to handle one million bits of information. Your brain can handle a billion if it has to. Your MEA can build a computer. No computer can build a "you." How about that? So you see you can learn anything your MEA decides to learn. Of course if MEC or MEP is allowed to "mess up" your computer, you may not learn anything. So we have to watch "old Brainless" when we're doing serious thinking. You're using MEA when you are reading this book (Figure 11).

20

AT THE STORE

1

2

3

21

4

fig. 9

THE BILLION DOLLAR COMPUTER

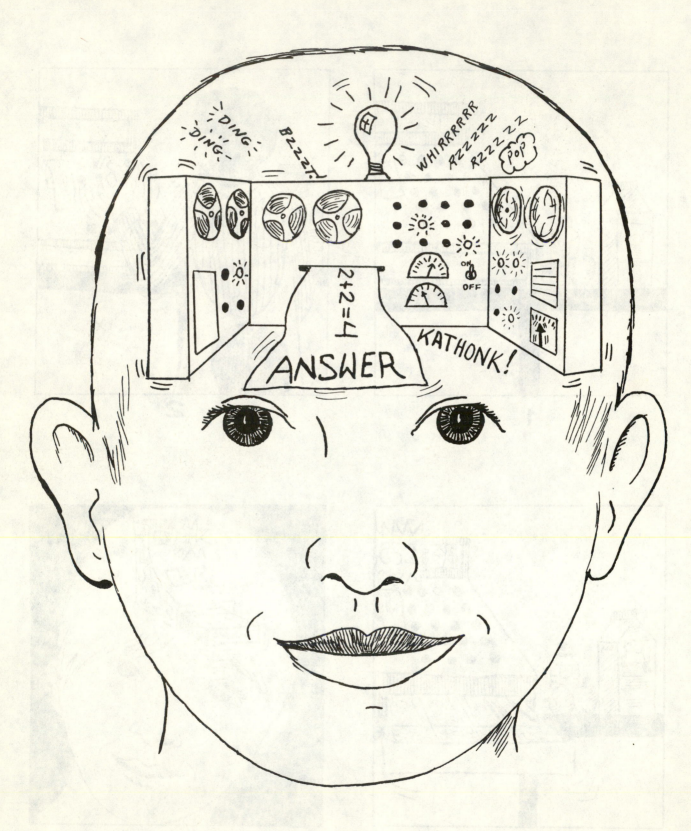

fig.10

MEA AT WORK

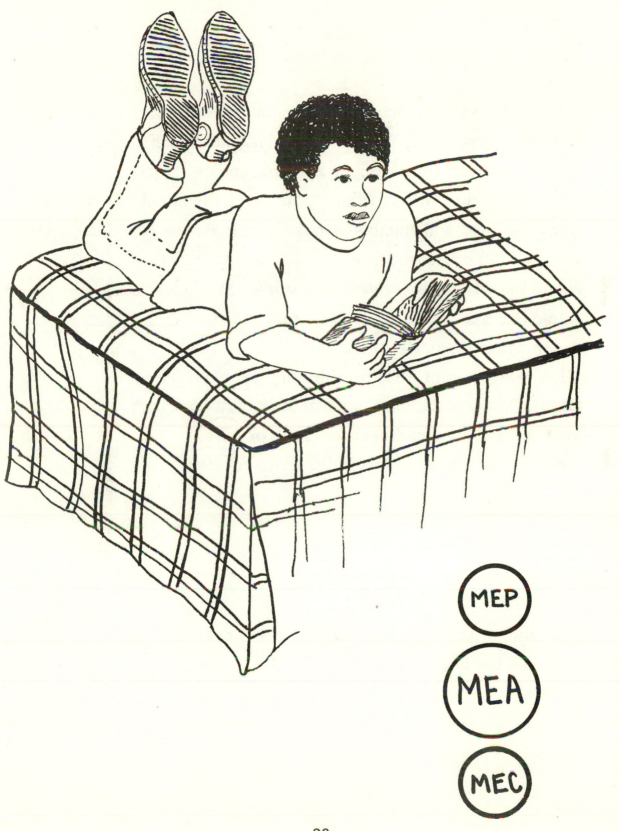

fig.11

Now let's see if you can tell when MEA, MEC or MEP is talking:

1. I hurt my toes, darn it. _C_
2. I'll put some mercurochrome and a bandage on it. _A_
3. That was a stupid thing I did — kicking that can. _P_

If you labeled #1 MEC, #2 MEA and #3 MEP you've been strengthening your MEA while you read. Number 1 was MEC expressing feelings and number 3 was Critical Parent (old MEP). Only MEA (number 2) made sense.

1. Name the one inside of you who thinks. _A_
2. Name the one inside of you who makes sense. _A_
3. A computer is smarter than MEA. True or ~~false~~.
4. MEA takes care of MEC by thinking. ~~True~~ or false.
5. Old Brainless is the name we call MEP. True or ~~false~~.
6. MEP works like a cash register. True or ~~false~~.
7. MEA works like a tape recorder. True or ~~false~~.

(To find out if you have labeled them correctly turn to page 80 and you'll see the answers.)

24

CHAPTER V — HOW TO KNOW WHO'S IN CHARGE

In Chapter II we spoke of the part of us called the Parent. "Children should be seen and not heard," is an old Parent saying. It's like something on a tape recorder. Old sayings are like that. (Sayings which you learned from Mother, Dad or other grown-ups like, "Always respect your elders," or "Children should be seen and not heard.") They are called Parent Tapes. What are some of your Parent Tapes? Tell three now. Mother and Daddy learned theirs from their mother and father and now you've learned some from them. They're part of your *Parent*. They're the bossy you and the kind you. At the right time Parent tapes help you. Sometimes your Child doesn't know what to do. Then your Parent tape tells you. The Parent is a good part of you. Sometimes though MEP makes your Child feel very uncomfortable. Especially when it won't let MEC do what he wants. At those times you can tell which part of you is the strongest. Who is the strongest in you? Who decides what you do? Discuss that right now. Later in Chapter X we'll learn more about Parent tapes which are bad for us.

There are four ways of knowing who is "the one" in you. First of all *you know how you feel!* Do you feel angry, hurt, sad or happy? Does something taste or smell good? If so you know which one is in charge. Who? Right, it's your Child.

A second way to know who is running things is *by the words you use.* If you're saying "wow," "umhum," "yippie," "heck," "darn," "thud," "pow," "biff," "aw shucks," etc. then that's your Child speaking. If you're using words like Mother and Daddy used, to tell you what you shouldn't do, like "stop that" or "you're filthy" or "you're dirty" or "that's nasty" or "that's a no-no," then *your* Parent is talking. If you're using words like "better," "more desirable," "nicer," "easier" then it's your Adult.

A third way to know who is "in charge" is to *figure out how you cause other people to act.* If others are coming on *MEP* you can bet your *MEC* is in charge of you. When that happens you "hook" their Parent (Figure 12).

Now why is it important to know all this? If I can find out which one of me is boss I can have a lot more fun, make a lot more sense and please the people around me. I can also know something about them and may not have as much trouble talking to them and letting them know how I feel. This is pretty important to me because when I try to talk to people now I often find that I can't get them to listen. My mother is always telling me that when she talks to me I sometimes don't seem to hear her. Maybe it's because the ME she talks to is turned off.

EXERCISES IN STROKING

Here are some exercises to try out on your little sister or brother or even Mother or Daddy. 1) Tell someone something nice about himself and watch him smile. You'll be stroking his Child (MEC). 2) Another exercise in stroking (doing a nice thing) is to be sure and call five people by their names today — people that you don't really know

PARENT HOOKING

fig.12

and watch what happens when you say their name. 3) Also, if you want to find out how it feels to get strokes, get four or five people to call you by your name. 4) If you really want to have fun touch some people that you like and get them to touch you. These exercises are for your Adult with fun for your Child. You'll find that you'll enjoy them. 5) Another exercise is to try to play detective and find your own Parent. Listen to what you say and when you find yourself being bossy, remark to yourself, "Uh huh, I sound like Daddy or Mother," or whoever it is that says things like that. Then you'll find that you're in your Parent, that MEP is talking. Once in a while you may even exercise your Adult, perhaps. Ask something that makes sense like, "When will dinner be ready?" See if you get an Adult answer. If it sounds like this, "You're always hungry," that would be Mother's Parent talking to your Child. So you see you can do a lot of things right now with just the little knowledge you have to find out about yourself and other people and learn how to get along with them better. That's what this book is all about.

Oh yes, there's one other thing I wanted to talk about. Sometimes one of the three people inside me gets messed up by the others. It is sort of like when you put your fingers in your ears and then you can't hear. This happens when one of the people, like the Child or Parent, is very much in charge and doesn't want to hear anything else. If the Child hears what Mother has to say, it'll make the Child stop what it's doing. For example, sometimes when I was reading, Mother would say, "Al, will you get up and clean your room?" My Child didn't want to hear that so MEC would say, "I don't hear anything, I don't want to hear anything and I want to keep on reading." That messing up of the

Adult (Figure 13) so that the message doesn't get through is called a big word that you don't have to remember unless you want to. It's called contamination, con-tam-i-nation. You can say it if you can read it, con-tam-i-nation. All it means is "messed up." Like smeared with mud so that you can't really see the person. But that "messing up" sometimes messes up the way we learn to talk to each other. Because if I am angry my Adult is messed up and I can't hear you asking me to go to a party. I may say something out of my childlike anger that has nothing to do with your question. That's why sometimes we have to take a look and find out what our Kid is doing. Sometimes it messes up all of the fun we can have with other people.

Now today we have learned some new things about ourselves. We have learned that there are three people inside of us. We call them "Parent," "Adult" and "Child." These three people are very real. They have names and addresses. They express our feelings, the bossy part of us, and the part that makes sense. Any one of them can be messed up or knocked out by any one of the others. When that happens we can't hear what other people are saying to us. Then we use what we feel or what we believe to make our decisions. This means that we can't understand other people nor they us. That's what gets us into trouble. In the rest of the chapters of this book we'll try to find out how to do better than that so that we're happier every day.

CHILD CONTAMINATED ADULT

fig.13

EXERCISES FOR GROUP

1. Four ways of knowing who is speaking (P-A-C)
   a. You know how you _feel_ .
   b. You know by the _way x words_ you speak.
   c. You can tell who is speaking in you by the way _others react_ _____ towards you.
   d. You can tell by how you _listen& act_ .

2. Sayings we learned from Mother and Father before we were five years old (like "children must obey their parents") are called _parent_ _tapes x_ .

3. The three people inside us, Parent, Adult and Child, are real; they have names and addresses. (True) or false.

4. When Mother tells me it's time to go to bed and I don't "hear" her it's probably because my 1) _Adult_ . is messed up by my 2) _Child_ .

5. Try to stroke somebody's Child right now by saying or doing something to them. You'll know if you do by their pleased look.

(To find out if you have labeled them correctly turn to page 80 and you'll see the answers.)

CHAPTER VI — STROKES

Have you noticed how cats and dogs like to be petted, stroked, fed, played with and talked to? You and I are the same way. When we were little we were petted, touched, talked to and played with by Mom and Dad and these actions felt good. They pleased me. I call those actions which give me those pleasant feelings "strokes" (Figure 14).

A hand on my shoulder is a stroke. A hug is a stroke. "Hello!" is a stroke. Sometimes someone does something to me which is unpleasant, like a slap. That can be a stroke, too. An unpleasant stroke. But all strokes stir you up. If you don't get them, you'll get sick. Strokes are like food. We must have them and once we get them we will do anything for more of them.

A friend of mine calls strokes that feel good "warm fuzzies."* He calls strokes that hurt "cold pricklies." Sometimes, when we think we can't get a "warm fuzzy," we will work to get a cold prickly. Any stroke is better than no stroke.

Do you ever work to get a cold prickly? (To get a spanking.) One time doctors and nurses in a big hospital discovered that babies that were not being stroked because nobody lifted or cuddled them or cooed over them got sick. They seemed to give up wanting to live, and

*Reference: Steiner, Claude M. PhD., Transactional Analysis Bulletin, Vol. 9, No. 36, October, 1970.

EVERYBODY NEEDS STROKES

baby

son

mom and dad

grampa and grandma
fig. 14

some stopped living. At the same time, the doctor discovered that the babies who were cuddled and stroked grew strong and healthy. From that time on the doctor told the nurses to stroke the babies. All the babies were stroked and nobody got sick.*

Do you like strokes? I do — what's your favorite "warm fuzzy?" How do you like to be stroked — a back rub, smile, an "A" or what? Talk about it to your mother today. Talk about it now.

When we're little babies we need to be touched often. Touching makes us go. We've already learned that if babies don't get strokes they may get sick and die. We never stop needing strokes. Later we learn to like smiles, kind looks and words (like "good"). They're strokes, too! A friend of mine says stroking is best when it's for being. Most often parents give us strokes for doing. Later we'll learn what happens when we think we can't do what others expect of us.

If I don't get strokes, I feel bad. When I get strokes, I feel good.

Any stroke is better than no stroke. Strokes from spanking, yelling, name calling and bossing are cold pricklies but they are better than no strokes. "Cold pricklies" are better than no "warm fuzzies." Sometimes, when I think nobody loves me (will give me strokes), I try to make them mad — at least I'll get them to know I'm there and they'll stroke me (even though it hurts).

*Reference: Berne, Eric, M.D., Games People Play, Grove Press, 1964

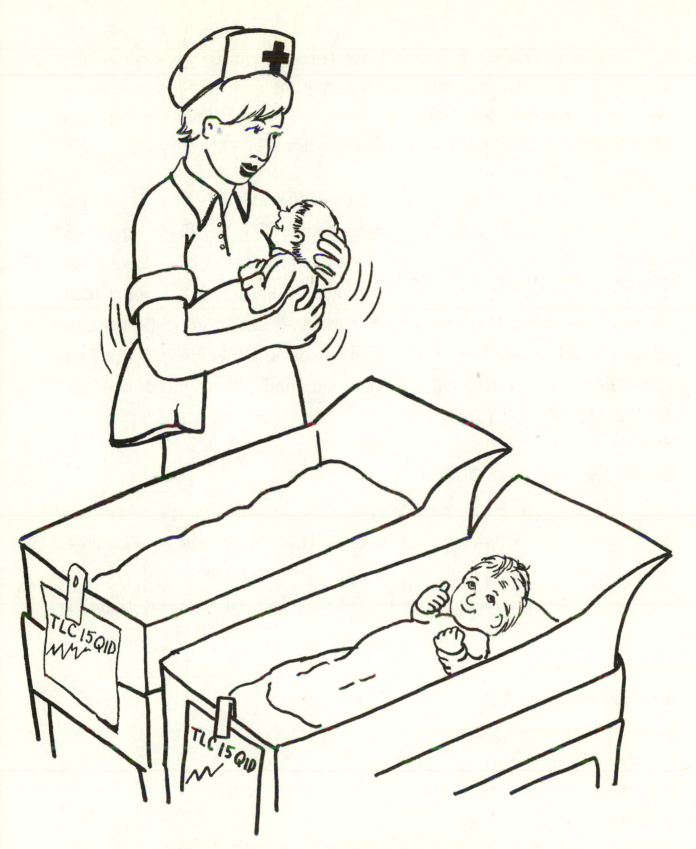

**Tender Loving Care
15min., 4 Times a Day**

35

fig·14a

The strokes that I like best are friendly words, my own name, somebody to touch me, rub my back, hug me and even kiss me (if not too often or too sloppy). How do you get strokes? What kind do you like? Dislike? Talk about it now for a few minutes.

To have very few strokes or no strokes at all is like not living. Some strokes are given to me because people like me. These I get free. When I don't get strokes for free, I do things to get strokes. Like I will help someone and they will thank me. "Thank you," is an earned stroke. Sometimes I will bug mother or sister until they yell at me or hit me. These things hurt but they are strokes. Other times I will be a good boy and they will tell me that I am good. What I need most are the free strokes, just for being me.

EXERCISES FOR GROUP

In this chapter you have learned about strokes, good strokes, hurt strokes, earned strokes and free strokes. How do you get your strokes? Talk about this. What kind do you get most? From whom? Who do you like getting strokes from? How come? What do you do to get them? Is this the best way?

1. What is a stroke?
2. Why do we need strokes?
3. What kinds of strokes are there?
4. What is a free stroke?
5. Tell how to earn strokes.
6. Give somebody in group a free stroke.
7. Are all strokes pleasant?

CHAPTER VII — STAMP COLLECTIONS

Does your family save Green Stamps or Blue Chip Stamps? What do you do with them? That's right, you stick them in a book until it is full and then you can get something good that you want for free. Lots of people save stamps in books. When the book is full it can be turned in for something they want. They get a free prize.

My Child (MEC) likes to put Blue Chip Stamps in a book and dream about what they'll bring when the book is full (Boy, maybe I'll get a motorcycle). MEP likes this, too, because I believe I am saving money, even if MEA says I'm not.

MEC collects other kinds of stamps. We'll call these TA brown stamps. Whenever I get my feelings hurt, get afraid or get mad and I keep those mean feelings inside, I am saving TA brown stamps. Saving brown stamps is saving up feelings to trade in for strokes that I feel I've got coming to me. Just like when I trade in the Blue Chip Stamps I get a free prize. If I save enough anger, sometime I'm going to have a temper tantrum or a fight (anger without feeling guilty is the "free prize"). That will happen perhaps when I least expect it over some little thing that really doesn't mean anything. Did that ever happen to you? It's sort of like putting in one more stamp to fill the book and then you can get your free prize all at once.

The secret of brown stamps is that they are printed inside you and me. When MEP calls MEC "stupid," MEC prints a brown stamp and that's a saved stroke. Then I either throw it away or put it in a stamp book.

MEC can do three things with brown stamps. He can keep them and save them up for a big explosion; throw them away as soon as they are printed or not print them at all.

Here is a story of how I might get some brown stamps. I am on my way to school and I see John, who is a friend of mine, walking with a girl (Figure 17) who is a friend of his. So I say to him, "Hi, John," and John walks right on by and doesn't say anything. I have strokes coming to me from John so I put two brown stamps in my "feeling" book. Later on in class Mary leans over and asks for a pencil. I start to tell her that I do not have one. The teacher sees me and bawls me out for speaking during class, so I don't say anything, but I put away another brown stamp. That was so unfair to get blamed and not be able to tell anyone. Later on somebody else at home asks me to do something; turn off the TV or run an errand, and I explode all over the place about how everybody picks on me and nobody likes me, all they want to do is use me and so on, and everybody wonders why I am so upset. Of course, I don't remember to tell them about Johnny and Mary. All I do is unload on them because it's safer at home. So, anyway, you can say that I traded in my brown stamps for a big temper tantrum at home. Some prize, a temper tantrum — felt good to let it out but everybody else felt bad.

Now I was thinking about brown stamps. The only way that somebody can give you some, "make you angry," is when your MEP or Parent agrees with them and your Adult doesn't stop the brown stamp printing machine. OK? Now what can you do about brown stamps. Well, MEC and MEA can throw brown stamps away. Again, MEC can say, "Hey, John, I spoke to you, didn't you hear me?" Or MEA can say, "Well, maybe John doesn't want to talk to me now. He's busy talking to Wendy. I'll see him later. I don't have to get worried about it or angry." Later on in the Mary incident I can say to myself, "Well, I can protect Mary. Really, it's not going to hurt anybody and I guess the teacher's kind of upset about the noise in the room, so I'll just keep quiet and forget it. I'm OK and she's OK." Later on if I have picked up any stamps, I can talk about it to Mary. I'll tell her how mad I got when it happened, that I'm not angry with her and guess the teacher had a right to tell me about it. So brown stamps can be printed or not printed. Brown stamps can be saved or thrown away. What do you do with brown stamps? Do you have any today? Let's talk about them and maybe we can tell you how you can go about getting rid of them.

CHAPTER VIII — GAMES YOU PLAY

Do you like to play games? I do. What games do you enjoy the most? Talk about that for a minute. Do you like hopscotch, baseball, hide and seek, cops and robbers? What do you like to play? Most people, when they are little, like to play some sort of game. Sometimes boys and girls like to play with dolls and keep house. Other times they like to play running games. Later on they like to build models. There are so many different kinds of games to play. And they're all for fun. Flying a kite is fun. Did you ever fly a kite with the wind blowing through your hair, and you skimming along down hill? The excitement of the thing pulling strokes your Child, doesn't it? Makes you feel great, excited.

Lots of games that we play are to win something. We must either run faster or further than someone else to win a prize, get applause or approval from people we like. So, winning is a way of getting strokes and it is one of the reasons we try to win. (Figure 16) We also play to fill in the time and keep from being bored. You've heard people say, "Oh, I'm bored. Let's play_____." That means that their Child isn't having any fun. They feel very dull and their MEC is restless.

When MEC is not getting any strokes he gets unhappy and scared. "Maybe I won't get any strokes," he thinks. As a result people sometimes begin to play a kind of TA game that I want to talk about

fig. 16

today. The TA games that they play are designed to get them strokes or make other people give them strokes, which they don't feel they can get any other way. You know why? Because they don't think they're OK. They don't think these other people love them enough to give them free strokes. Then, because their Child is hurting, bored, angry or scared, they begin to play transactional games to force others to stroke them. Now this is a different kind of game than the athletic game or the kite flying.

Let me tell you how it goes. Here's an example of a game with a funny name. "Schlemiel." It's a German word for somebody who is clumsy. The game goes like this: You invite Joe to visit you. You're sitting at the table and he spills his milk. He offers to clean it up and knocks over his chair and the ash tray. He grabs the cloth and knocks over and breaks one of mother's good dishes. Then he says, "I'm sorry." Another time he gets up to give somebody his chair and knocks the chair over and breaks it. Again, "I'm sorry, please forgive me." After he's done this on six different visits, each time accidentally breaking or spilling something you and mother begin to wonder why. The secret lies in how you behaved. Remember the first time he spilled the milk? What did Mother do? She said, *Oh! That's all right.* (Figure 17) Here I'll clean it up and *here's another glass for you.*" In other words she forgave him. Well, Joe who, doesn't get too many free strokes at home, feels he has to "earn" strokes. So he plays Schlemiel, a game which results in several kinds of rewards - the excitement and fun of breaking things, the attention he gets, the anger and then the

a game of "SCHLEMIEL"

fig.17

forgiveness which says, "no matter what you do you're OK." Maybe it would be easier to tell him first (but first put the good china away) that he's OK no matter what he does. Sometimes kids play Schlemiel just to make a mess and to get negative strokes. How can they lose?

Now there is another game that lots of people play. It is called "What'll I do? Why don't you? Yes but." If you'll listen in group or at home you'll hear people play this. It goes like this: It: "What'll I do about my brother? He is always taking my things." Someone might say, "Well, why don't you share things with him?" "It" says, "Well, yes, but he won't stick to the agreement." Then someone else may say, "Well, then you could just let him have whatever he wants and agree that you can have his things when you want them." "Yes but he won't give them to me," "It" says. Then someone may come back with, "Well, you could put a lock on the door." "Yes but my mother won't let me." So on goes the game until the group gives up. Then "It" has won! His MEC has put the group's MEPs down. He has proven that the doctor doesn't know any more about his problems than he does. Therefore he now has added reason for finding fault with his brother. A good reason for doing what he wants to do. There's no other way. Even the doctor doesn't know one. Asking the questions, asking for help, then showing the other person why what he suggests is no good, is a game.

Remember, a game has four parts. The four parts are: the "hook," "maneuver," "gimmick" and "payoff." In the "What'll I do? Why don't you? Yes but. (YB)" game the "hook" is "I've got a problem, what'll I

45

do?" the "maneuver" is to get the person to make suggestions. Then the "gimmick" is never to let them win, never to take their suggestions and always to tell 'em why they won't work (put down). The "payoff" is in defeating that person (or group), putting him down and proving that he doesn't know what he is talking about. We like to do this to older people like Mother, Dad, teacher or older brother or someone whom you see as pretty bossy. This is your way of cutting them down. After a while we do it to everyone so we'll feel OK. Now the one thing about a game that makes it a game is that *you don't know you are playing it.* Your Kid (MEC) plays it for satisfaction and strokes but your Adult isn't aware of it. Your Adult would know it doesn't make much sense to put somebody down but your Kid is frantic to get strokes because it doesn't figure it will get them free.

Talk about games. Find out if you play games. Here are some that are famous because they are played so often. You'll recognize them from their opening "hook" or close off.

"Ain't it awful"

"See what you made me do"

"If it weren't for you"

"Now I've got you"

"Kick me"

"Stupid"

"Wooden leg" (Wooden head)

"Uproar"

"Let's you and him fight"

"Blemish"

and a whole lot of others and most of all "Cops and robbers." So, let's talk about these at our next meeting.

By the way, can you tell who is playing these games (P, A or C) from the title? Label them now and see if you agree with others in the group. Tell why you thought they were MEA, MEP or MEC playing.

CHAPTER IX — RACKETS

Today I would like to talk about rackets. We often hear about gangs that are stealing things or about gamblers that are in the racket. Their racket is to get money in ways that are against the law. They cheat. Sometimes in growing up in a family we learn the family racket for getting strokes. We learn to copy how the family gets its stamps. How Grandpop or Uncle go about getting their strokes. Sometimes we watch "Mother and Dad" feel sad and we learn how to be sad. If they do that often we are learning the family racket; the family racket of collecting brown stamps and the kind of stamps to like. These rackets destroy good feelings towards ourselves and towards other people. We learn to collect special kinds of stamps, to trade them in or to dump them on other people. We learn how to hurt others and to feel good about it. You know, "getting back at them" for example is a game intended to get us NIGY* stamps. Sometimes we save up brown stamps until we feel that we've got too many and we're entitled to hurt someone or something. When we hit someone we have unloaded a lot of saved up insults and hurts so that they hurt like we do. This is supposed to make us feel better but all it does is cause us to lose a friend or hurt someone. We might also do some damage to someone we love which would make us feel guilty. "Guilty" is a combination of anger (red) and fear (blue) stamps. We've been taught not to let our anger out. When we

*Now I Got You

feel anger but don't show it we print "red" stamps. All of them make us feel lousy (dark brown). So in cashing in your stamps even if you do it the way Mom or Dad did it you can feel pretty unhappy (blue).

Sometimes when we feel we don't get enough love at home we go shopping for stamps. Sometimes we set-up someone to give us stamps. We don't think we rate free strokes (gold) so we have to "con" (convince) them into *giving* us strokes. How do you do that? We might try a little game of "Yes, but." You know how that goes. "Dad, what can I do about being late for school?" "Well, you could get up earlier." "*Yes, but* I am too tired" (I win). We can keep that up, getting strokes all the time. The madder Dad gets the more strokes we get. Showing him how wrong he is sure gets him mad. Being late gets us more strokes. We win three ways. We get to stay in bed; we put Dad down and, of course, we get negative strokes from teacher who bawls us out when we are late. So this, again, is a neat way of working the anger racket to get more strokes than we think we can get by coming on straight. That is by getting up and getting to school on time. And so today we learned about rackets, and how we use games to make the rackets work.

In some families kids learn how to get and give strokes. If they get more than they need they can save them for a sad day. What color are happy stamps?

Now here's a little quiz for you whiz kids. Not that you'll need them but the answers I give are at the end of this book.

1. A racket is a family's way of getting strokes. ~~True~~ or false.
2. Boys and girls learn the family racket in school. True or ~~false~~.
3. Kids can learn to collect "happy" stamps if they're shown how by their family. ~~True~~ or false.
4. "NIGY" is a game of ___Now I got you___ .
5. "Happy" stamps are colored ___Yellow Gold___
6. "Angry" stamps are colored ___Red___ .
7. "Sad" stamps are colored ___Blue___ .
8. "Guilty" stamps are colored ___Red___ and ___Blue___ .
9. All bad stamps are colored ___Brown___ .
10. Best stamps are colored ___Gold___ .

(To find out if you have labeled them correctly turn to page 80 and you'll see the answers.)

CHAPTER X — PARENT POISON (PP's)*

Did the doctor ever give you a shot? Ouch! Hurts doesn't it? (And why do they always do it *there?*) Well, today we're going to talk about taking TA *SHOTS* to prevent NOK which is caused by Parent Poison (PP). Medical doctors give shots to keep you from getting sick. For example they give vaccinations against smallpox or polio, sicknesses caused by poison virus. TA is a shot which fights off Parent Poisons and prevents the dread NOK disease. Parent Poisons are the words mothers and fathers use when we're very little which result in our getting the "Not OK" (NOK) Disease. Once we get this dread disease (feel Not OK) we become carriers and go around giving it to other people like smaller brothers and sisters or friends or, later on, our own children.

No one means to give others NOK. You don't and your mother and father didn't. They love you. My mother and dad loved me. But they got the "Not OK" disease from their folks and gave it to me. Now we TAers know how to stop NOK, how to get rid of it and how to prevent its spread. Wouldn't it be great if no one ever had the NOK disease again? You can help prevent it, get rid of your own and never give it to anyone else. Isn't TA terrific? Here's how.

*The ideas here were suggested in a paper presented by Kenneth Ernst
at the Golden Gate Spring Conference, 1971.

THE NOK DISEASE:

People with NOK go around always feeling not OK. They're sad or angry or hurt and they don't know why. They carry brown stamps around looking for someone or something to dump them on. Some people dump them on things. I know a girl who was so full of BS (Brown Stamps) she used to pull her hair out. How come? Well, one of her PP's was, "Don't you dare show your anger. Keep it to yourself." So when she got angry she turned her anger on herself. Another person I know, a very nice person now, got angry at his dad and set fire to a neighbor's car. He didn't want to hurt anyone but he wanted to get his anger out. His PP was, "Don't you give me any of your back talk." Some other PP's are: "Don't feel," "Don't think," "Don't grow up, stay a little girl (be my baby)," "Be stupid," "Be stubborn," "Stutter," "Be afraid," "Be second (be a loser)," "Be lazy (you're just like your Uncle Joe, the laziest man on earth)." OK? Get the idea what PP's are?

The onset (as doctors say) of the NOK disease begins with the first NOK message. It gets worse with time because the more you try to do what Parent tells you to do, the stronger the poison they give you. "You're just plain lazy." "You're born lazy." "I'll punish you for *be*ing lazy." (Be lazy, you're born lazy, doomed to be lazy all your life.)

THE PREVENTION AND CURE:

Spotting Parent Poisons is an Adult activity. When you see, hear or feel one coming at you you can alert your MEC not to take it. Then MEC doesn't take the poison and doesn't feel NOK. One way to become an expert NOK spotter is to listen to mothers and fathers talking to their children. Another way is to talk about PP's in group. Here are some I just heard. "My Jamie is so stubborn." (Be stubborn.) "You're just a little thief." (Be a thief.) "You're a clown." "Isn't he a clown, Mommy?" "Yes, dear! But he's so cute." (PP — Be a clown.) Which ones have you heard? Talk about them now.

TA SHOTS:

TA is like a shot against PP. TA makes you able to recognize Parent Poison instantly and duck so it won't hurt. The minute you hear one it is quite easy to duck. Of course you must be in your MEA to avoid taking any PP. Follow up with a P shrinker. Give three straight strokes to the P's Kid and watch the Parent Poisoner fade into smiles. Strokes are infectious, too. But it's a nice cure and gets you gold stamps.

EXERCISE FOR GROUP!

1. Have you heard any PP's? Tell us about them.
2. Let's make up a play with somebody being a son or daughter. MP and FP give out PP's and son and daughter spot, duck and shrink P's.
3. What is NOK disease?
4. How can you keep from getting NOK disease?
5. How can you get rid of it?

CHAPTER XI — PROMISES, AGREEMENTS AND CONTRACTS

Did somebody ever promise to bring you something? Wasn't that fun? They said, "When I come home I'm going to bring you a new toy," or even more exciting, "I'm going to *bring you something.*" When they came home from their trip, after some delay they said, "Oh, yes, I promised to bring you something and I did." (Figure 17a) What fun that was and you learned that "promise" meant "You can trust me." Then another time they promised to bring you something and they didn't. They said, "Oh, I forgot." Wow, wasn't that awful? On still another occasion they said, "I'll bring you something," and you said, "Will you promise?" and they said, "I promise." Then you said, "Do you always keep your promises?" and this person said, "I always keep my promises. I do what I say I will do." Now you knew that they were going to bring you a gift because they said they *always keep* their promises. Since they always keep their promises you knew you could depend on them to do what they said they would do. In the same way when you make a promise, people know you'll do what you say. Promising is very, very important. Keeping your promise is even more important if you want people to believe you. Have you ever made a promise? Tell about it right now.

Have you ever heard of grown-ups saying, "I have a new contract with the firm," or "Willie Mays just signed a new contract?" What they

PROMISES, PROMISES...

fig.17a

are talking about is a grown-up way of putting down on paper what they promise to do for each other. They sign a paper saying they agree to do so much work for a certain amount of money. Promises are important because if people are not able to trust each other then everything gets mixed up, people get confused and disappointed and no one knows what to do. To get away from getting mixed up like that the best idea is for people to say exactly what they intend to do and do it. Next, let the other person know what they want the other person to do. Then, if both agree, they can make a contract which will keep them from being mixed up. Saying you're going to do something is one thing. Doing it is the important thing. Both are very necessary parts of a contract.

Now, how do contracts work at home? Do you have any contracts? We do. At our house there are two boys, my wife and I. A long time ago we made a contract that on Monday, Wednesday and Friday evenings Mark (whose name begins with an M) would do the dishes. (Figure 18) On Tuesday, Thursday and Saturday Larry would do the dishes and on Sunday I would do them. Mother does the cooking so she "gets out" of dishes. That contract worked out pretty well and we never argue about dishes. What kind of a contract do you have about doing the dishes at your house or about coming home from school, about keeping your room clean or shining the car? Talk about them right now.

FAMILY CONTRACTS

fig.18

One thing that makes a contract work is that you have a part in deciding how it is going to work and feeling it's fair and agreeing to it. You see, when we made the contract about the dishes, we sat down around the table and agreed about the best way to get the dishes done. We all agreed on the arrangement I just told you about. We felt it was the best and fairest one for us. That way nobody felt that they were cheated and everybody kept the contract.

Sometimes mothers or fathers just tell us what to do. They say, "Now here's the way it's going to be." Then we don't feel that we have a part in it and we feel sort of cheated. We feel it's not fair and we're not really in agreement. We didn't really promise. We were told what to do. So, if the contract is going to work, it's better if the people who agree to it should help build it. Sometimes it doesn't work out for one reason or another. Rather than letting MEP say, "You broke your contract," you can go back and change the plan. "Well, this didn't work because . . . so, isn't there some other way?" Then you can rework it so that everybody can keep their contract promises.

One last word on promises and trust. Just because you or someone else does not *always* keep a promise does not mean people can never trust them again. Sometimes things keep people from doing what they say. Other times they just forget. Did you ever forget your promise? Do you always forget your promise? Do you remember 90% (9 times out of 10), 80% of the time? Guess I'd trust you most of the time. Nobody's perfect nor perfectly awful. Somewhere in between lies the truth.

When people grow up they may forget about how important promises are. They break some very serious ones. You may have heard of the word divorce. Well, lots of times divorces occur when people don't keep their promises to each other.

When promises (treaties) between countries are broken it sometimes leads to war and killing. So, agreements and promises are very important and they make contracts work.

In TA we try to make contracts very, very clear. We ask people to say what they want to get by learning TA. What are you going to work on? What are you going to accomplish; what are you going to change in you? If you can say that, then I can help you to accomplish your goal. The contract between us is clear. Now will you take the time to figure out what kind of contract you have with me? At home? At school?

1.   A promise is a contract. True or false.

2.   An agreement is a contract. True or false.

3.   Tell why promises are important to you.

4.   Tell why keeping your promises is important to you.

5.   What happens when you or someone else fails to keep their promises? Did this ever happen to you? Tell about it. How did you handle it — P, A or C? What could you have done about it so that everybody came out a winner?

6.   Talk about trusting people. Whom do you trust? Why? Did you ever trust someone and they let you down? Could you trust them again? What do you think about when you stop trusting people?

7.   Let's do some trust exercises.

(To find out if you have labeled them correctly turn to page 80 and you'll see the answers.)

CHAPTER XII — HOW YOU AND I SPEAK TO EACH OTHER!

Have you ever said "Hello" to someone and they didn't answer you? How did you feel? You felt cheated, right? Well, you were and you got some stamps. When you said, "Hello, Marge," (Figure 19) (or whatever the person's name was) you were giving them strokes and you were not getting any back. So you had some coming. The stamp is a *record* of what's owed to you. At another time you may have asked, "Mother, are you home?" (Figure 20) Mother said, "Yes, dear, I'm in here." In this case you felt good because she answered you. Not only that but she gave you some extra strokes. Which ones were extra? (Right, "Yes, dear.") In the first case, you had an incomplete transaction. In the second one, you had a complete transaction, one that was complete or finished. You gave some strokes and you got some back. In the second transaction, the one you had with mother (Figure 20) you notice how the arrows go from your MEA to her MEA and how her arrow goes from her MEA to your MEA. Have you ever asked, "Mother, may I go out?" She says, "Have you finished your work?" Now, what happened there? That's right, you asked from your Adult to her Adult, "Mother, may I go out?" and she came on from her Parent to your Child. That was a cross transaction which made you unhappy and added some brown stamps. (Figure 21)

INCOMPLETE TRANSACTION

2 Strokes
− 0 Strokes
= 2 Brown Stamps

fig. 19

A PARALLEL TRANSACTION

fig. 20

A CROSS TRANSACTION

fig. 21

As you can tell from the above little stories, there are at least two different ways to talk to people. One is where people are able to make themselves understood and get an answer that makes sense. Like this: my MEA says, "How are you?" and your MEA says, "Fine." (Figure 20)

The other one is a cross transaction and here the lines cross, like an X and it doesn't make sense. That's when we begin to have trouble between people. (Figure 21)

What I'm going to talk about today are transactions (T) and the effect they have on you. You know, ever since you were born you've been having transactions (T) with people. Everytime you talk to someone or they speak to you or you answer them, or you see them do something and you answer them you're having a transaction (T). The record in your brain of all those "T's" makes up all the things that you are as a person.

When you were little the first transactions you had with Mother and Dad formed your Child (MEC) and your Parent (MEP). Every transaction you have ever had was recorded and you never forgot it. If you wanted to you could remember whatever happened to you from the time you were a baby. The very important and painful transactions we tend to remember. Like the time I burned my finger. How it hurt. Or the time Mother told me I must *share* things with my cousin

Leonard and I didn't want to. I remember that because the whole thing was so unpleasant. We remember the feelings but we often can't remember what it was all about. Somebody says, "I got a spanking one time. Boy! I'll never forget it." And I say, "What was it for?" They reply, "Oh, I don't know. Something I did." We remember the spanking but we don't remember the reason. Sometimes a transaction is sneaky. We say one thing but mean something else. For example, you may say to your sister while grown-ups are busy talking, "Hey, sis, let's go out and play in the yard." And your sister says, "Okay, let's go." Really what you're saying is, "Hey, sis, these grown-ups are boring, let's get away from them." And Sister knows what you mean and says, "Okay, let's." If you were to draw a diagram, it would look like Figure 22. We call this a dual transaction or a double one. Sometimes dual transactions occur without our MEA knowing it. Then it's hidden (ulterior).

The most important transaction is the parallel. Do you think you can remember that one? It goes like this, "How are you today, Bryan?" and the answer comes back, "I'm fine." Draw the lines and arrows in Figure 23 and label them. The reason that this kind of transaction is important is because it's the one that helps us to make sense and to understand other people.

A DOUBLE TRANSACTION

fig. 22

YOU PUT IN THE ARROWS

fig. 23

Now for today, let's see how many different kinds of transactions we can think up and write down. What kind have you had today in school, here in the group, at home, out on the playground? Can you tell the difference between a parallel, a cross and double transaction? Give an example of each and share them with us. Draw the diagrams and see if you can make them clear to yourself and to other people with the use of the lines and circles. You'll find that it is a lot of fun to figure out who is saying what to whom and what they mean by it. If you can't figure it out and you get stuck, bring it to group and maybe your leader and the group can figure it with you.

Here are some first lines. You fill in the second.

1. When you say, "Hello," to someone you are giving them a _____.

2. If they do not say, "Hello," to you you feel cheated. You pick up or print one _____ _____ .

3. A brown stamp is a _____ of a stroke owed to you.

4. A stroke is a "feeling of being loved" given to you by _____.

5. When you speak to someone from your MEA to their MEA and they answer you the same way you have a _____ transaction.

6. When you speak to one ME (A) in someone and they answer from another (C) you have a _____ transaction.

7. When a cross transaction happens you're most likely to have a ___ .

8. When two people speak at one level (like from A to A) but mean something else (like from C to C) they are having a _____ transaction.

To find out if you have labeled them correctly turn to **page 80** and you'll see the answers.)

CHAPTER XIII — I'M OK — YOU'RE OK

In several of the other chapters we've talked a great deal about strokes. We learned that strokes are very important. If we don't get them when we're little, we get unhappy, may get sick or even die. We also learned that strokes are usually given to us for things that we do and we get the feeling that we have to earn them. Strokes are for doing (or not doing) what very important people, known as Mother and Dad, want us to do. Sometimes I like to feel that people give me strokes just because I'm me. I wish they would give them to me more often for that reason. Do you ever feel that way? That you would like to have strokes (like to be loved) just because you're you? And not because of what you do. Strokes make people feel good. They make them feel OK. "OK" means "worth something, able and important." You're able to think, you are important and you are worth a great deal. Do you feel OK? Yes? No? How did you get that feeling? How did you get a feeling of "not OK"? Talk about that now. How can you change from feeling "not OK" to feeling "OK"?

When you were born you were "OK." Everybody is OK when they are born (worthwhile, able and important). They are worth more than anything else in the world to their mothers and fathers. Ask your mother and father how much they would sell you for. And while they may tease a little and say, "Just make me an offer," they wouldn't take any amount, not even a million billion dollars, for you. So you have worth, not just alone in money, although that's important, but you have worth just because you exist. Oh, I know they will tell you sometimes, "Go get lost," or even to "Go play on the freeway," but they don't mean it because you are important. You are a part of them. You count. Being able means able to think. There isn't one of you who isn't able to think enough to do what's required of you. You're *OK* means being worthwhile, being important to yourself and to others and being able to do what you need to do. Now everybody, and I mean *everybody*, is born OK. How come then that so many of us, you and I, often have feelings of being "not OK"? Well, here's the way it goes.

When you are first born, you're OK and you feel OK. Most mothers and daddies take good care of you, give you strokes and love you and hold you close and so on. Then you start to grow and they feel they must teach you what to do to be human. So they start giving you strokes for doing what they want you to do. And only if you do or don't do whatever they think is *right*. Now suppose it happens that you're not able to do what they want you to do when they want you to do it in the way that they want you to do it. Then they tell you what's wrong with you and how many things you're doing wrong and how bad you are and how nasty and mean and ugly and disobedient (that's a good word) or how "uncooperative" you are (that's another big word that you don't understand). Then at the ripe age of 2 you say to yourself, "Holy mackerel, what a mess I am. Nobody loves me. Nothing I do pleases anybody. I am just a failure. You know what, I couldn't

72

have gotten this way all by myself in this short space of time. It must be that I was born a mess or a failure. I'm not really OK and I never will be. I'm a born loser." Then you continue, "Now mother and dad, they know how to do everything right. So they and everybody else is OK. They're all important, worthwhile and adequate, but not me. *'I'm not OK. They are OK.'* Boy, that's a tough position to be in." Suddenly you realize that if you're "not OK" you won't get strokes. And you *need* strokes. You get scared because "if I'm not OK, nobody will love me, nobody will give me strokes and I'll *die.*" So you've got to do something right away to take care of that. And then you make a big decision at the age of 2 or 3. "Even though I'm not OK, I won't let anybody else know it. I'll keep a nice smile on my face and I'll be good and do what they want me to. That way they'll give me strokes and think I'm OK even though *I know I'm not.*" That decision, that you and I made a long time ago, is keeping us from feeling OK now. That little kid, 2 years old, made a decision that you and I are still believing. We're still letting that little child run our lives. Isn't that silly of us?

What are some of the "not OK" feelings you have? How can we get rid of them? How can we change from frogs or ugly ducklings into the prince or princesses that we really are now?

Remember — "YOU ARE OK." Say it, "I'm OK and You're OK" and that's the truth. (Figure 24) Now talk about it.

fig.24

CHAPTER XIV — ZOOM FREE WITH TA

Being OK is being free to live, to zoom to joy. We've been talking about getting acquainted with yourself, of getting to understand yourself and of how neat it would be if you were able to do this, because then you could rap with people and make it big.

You and I have learned a great deal about each other while we've been reading this book and talking about it together. We've learned how we are made up of three people. These three can talk to each other and to others. Sometimes when we talk we hurt or get hurt, we pick up stamps. Sometimes we play games and get mixed up. We learned about how there are family rackets. In the family we learned to be mad, sad or afraid as an "OK" way to feel. The other day a little girl told me she was afraid "people would get her." Later her mother told me the same thing about herself. Being afraid is their family racket.

We've learned that people are often unhappy unless they come on straight with each other. If they do that and they care about each other then they can begin to make more sense, get along better, love each other and to know that they are OK.

What I want to talk about today is how to make use of TA so that we can become skilled at making other people feel OK and in turn to feel OK. Here are some of the ways that I use TA. If other people are to feel good, I have to feel good. The first job then is to tell myself everyday, "I'm OK — You're OK." (Put a bumper sticker on your mirror and read it out loud every morning.) This means that other people are worthwhile, adequate and important and so am I. They won't hurt me and I won't hurt them. I can get close to them and love them and they can get close to me and love me. We can trust each other.

Remind yourself often that all people are OK. Mother and Daddy, brothers, sisters, playmates or teachers. Even people that are nasty to us are OK although sometimes they say some pretty angry things. That doesn't mean everything they do pleases me or everything I do pleases them. It only means that all of us are worthwhile, important and able to think. If we're able to do that we don't have to be angry with or afraid of each other.

TRACK DOWN FEELINGS AND AVOID BROWN STAMPS:

Wouldn't it feel better if you didn't have to sulk or go around feeling sad? The reason we do this is because we print and keep brown stamps. We talked about brown stamps earlier. One way to avoid printing brown stamps is to do what is called a "**trackdown.**"*As soon as your Child, MEC, feels uncomfortable do a trackdown.

You have seen the arrows that we have drawn to point out (that's a funny one, *to point out)* what happens to your Child when somebody shoots an arrow at you. They may say or do a mean thing and that hurts. So, in order not to take the red arrow which gets shot at you by somebody trying to hurt you or to put you down you can do what we

*Thanks to Larry Mart, Teaching Member, ITAA, Sacramento, California

call "trackdown." Here is the way it goes: As soon as you feel uncomfortable, as soon as someone says something that annoys you, as soon as someone does something that frightens you, you can say to yourself, *"I hurt,"* and then immediately say, *"How?"* The answer to this question puts you into your Adult. OK? The answer to "How?" is "anger," "fear" or "pain." The next question that you put to yourself is *"Which part? P, A or C?"* Usually the answer is my Child. Then you can ask, *"Who done it?"* (Like in a mystery play.) "Who done this to me?" The answer will be the person who sent the arrow like Joe or Dad, Mother, sister, brother or somebody. Then *"With what? (P, A or C?)"* Usually, if it is Mother or Dad, the answer is, "their Parent." OK? Then, *"Why did they do it?"* "Because they were afraid" or "because they were angry" or "because they were sad and their Child was unhappy and they were acting to protect me or something like that." So, stop to figure out what is going on. Now the next question is, *"What can I do now?"* The answer is, of course, "do a trackdown." This keeps you from getting angry, afraid or sad. Finally, *"What can I do different later?"* That's easy, "Avoid hooking other people." So there we have a "trackdown." Learn to do this in thirty seconds. It goes like this: *"I hurt. How? Which part? Who done it? With what? Why did he do it? What can I do different now? What can I do later?"*

By the time you get finished with the thirty-second trackdown you won't be angry, you won't be hurt, you won't be afraid and you won't print any brown stamps. You'll feel so much better because you didn't pick up any old, dilapidated, dirty, brown feelings.

KEEPING PEOPLE:*

Another way to use TA is to give lots of strokes to other people. You know, when we are growing up we are criticized a great deal. We're told by a lot of people what's wrong with us and so we learn to be criticizers. We are never really taught to tell other people how nice they are or about the good things they do or what we like about them. In fact, we get sort of embarrassed to hear it and we get embarrassed to tell it. If you practice, in group, telling other people what you like about them, what you admire, you'll find it is easier to do it at home. You'll find that other people begin to like you and like to be with you. There are other ways to "keep people." Look around and find something nice to tell each person in the group. Talk about how it felt to say it and how it felt to be told. How else can you stroke people? Talk about it right now.

Another way to use TA is to become more aware of the games that you get involved in. Do you start them or does somebody else? It's important to know how to get out of them. Did you ever get into a game of "Why don't you, yes, but?" How annoying when someone asks you to tell them something and then they tell you what's wrong with it. So, one way of getting out of that game is not to play. If they ask you what to do don't give advice and perhaps you won't be sucked into a game that winds up with you feeling very foolish. There are other games. Talk about those in group and find out how to get out of them. There are some good ways to break up games. One way is to "cross the

*From lectures by Larry Mart, Teaching Member, ITAA, Sacramento, California

transaction." If you don't know how that works, ask somebody in group. Talk about it in group, too, because it's a little hard to describe it completely in this short book. When we play games we waste time and lose friends. If we can keep from playing games, if we can begin to know that other people are OK and that you're OK, you will have learned to use TA. You will have learned how to make yourself and the people you love happy.

I hope you have enjoyed reading this book. Keep your Adult plugged in, let your Kid out and have fun. Now get on with living a full wonderful loving life because you know you are OK.

ANSWERS TO QUIZZES

Chapter I - Page 7

1. C	6. A	11. P	16. C
2. C	7. A	12. C	17. P
3. P	8. P	13. C	18. C
4. P	9. C	14. C	19. C
5. A	10. P	15. P	20. C

Chapter II - Page 14

1. Parent
2. a) Child   b) MEC
3. Parent
4.
5. a) P   e) P or C
   b) P   f) P
   c) A   g) C
   d) C   h) P

Chapter III - Page 19

1. True
2. messes (con-tam-i-nates)
3. con-tam-i-nation
4. True
5. True
6. True
7. True
8. Child

Chapter IV - Page 24

1. A
2. A
3. F
4. T
5. F
6. F (MEA works like a cash register, takes in everything and puts it in the right slot for future use.)
7. F (MEP works like a tape recorder. Mother and Daddy fill up the tapes with some good stuff sometimes.)

Chapter V - Page 31

1. a) acts   b) words
   c) others act d) feel
2. Parent tapes
3. True - All three of you live or lived somewhere.
4. 1) Adult   2) Child
5. Did it work?

Chapter IX - Page 50

1. T
2. F
3. T
4. Now I've got you
5. Gold - Save for a blue day.
6. Red (angry)
7. Blue (sad)
8. Red & Blue (angry & sad)
9. Brown
10. Gold

Chapter XI - Page 61

1. T
2. T
3. Make a contract clear.
   Trust people. Trust me.
4. People will trust me, like me.
5. Things get confused, scary.
   Can't trust anyone.

Chapter XII - Page 70

1. Stroke
2. Brown stamp
3. Record
4. someone
5. parallel
6. cross
7. fight
8. double

TA for KIDS

(...and grown-ups too......)

by Alvyn M. Freed Ph.D.

"TA for Kids" is the first of a series to present Transactional Analysis (TA) to boys and girls (and their important grown-ups) in short words and simple phrases. Simplicity makes it easier to use TA concepts everyday. I think children will find this useful. The text draws on Dr. Eric Berne's "TA in Psychoanalysis," his best selling "Games People Play" and Dr. Tom Harris' "I'm OK -You're OK" as well as on my experience in presenting these ideas to the members of my groups. The series, geared to different age and grade levels, will enable pupils, their mothers and fathers and their teachers to make sense to each other.

"TA for Kids" is intended to be used by boys and girls in grades III - VI. Efforts are made to stroke the Kid and feed the Adult. The book is written in such a way that it may be read by boys and girls or *to* them by grown-ups. In my groups the children enjoyed listening. Sometimes they would take turns reading aloud to each other. The tests and exercises at the close of each chapter have excited and delighted the youngsters and encouraged them to continue learning. When the book was used with groups of children in the seven to eleven range the children enjoyed listening to the chapter and participating in the post-chapter tests. Older boys and girls and grown-ups also profit from the book.

ORDER FORM – TEAR HERE

JALMAR PRESS, Inc., 391 Munroe Street, Sacramento, California 95815 – Telephone (916) 481-1134
Distributed to the trade by Price/Stern/Sloan Publishers, Inc., 410 N. La Cienega Boulevard,
Los Angeles, California 90048.

Please send me the items indicated below:

_____ "TA for Kids (and grown-ups, too)" paperback - $4.00 per copy, plus $.42 postage and handling.

_____ "TA for Kids (and grown-ups, too)" hardback (Buckram bound) $7.95 plus $.60 postage and handling.

_____ "Today I'm Okay" poster (from "TA for Tots," pg. 232) 18 x 22 - $2.00 each plus $.50 postage and handling.

NAME: _____

STREET: _____

CITY: _____

STATE: _____ ZIP: _____

Enclosed is my check for _____
Prices subject to change without notice.

TA for TOTS
(and other prinzes*)

by Alyn M. Freed Ph.D.

"TA for Tots (and other Prinzes)" is a second book in the series "TA for Everybody." "Tots" simplifies for pre-school youngsters the basic ideas of Eric Berne's Transactional Analysis. Our purpose is to tell children that they are OK, that they are indeed princes and princesses. "TA for Tots" is the first step in inoculating children against an environment which leads them into forming destructive life scripts.

*Women's Lib for princes and princesses.

"TA for Tots" is geared to the pre-school level. Older Prinzes will enjoy it, too. The book is written and illustrated in such a way that it may be read *by* youngsters or *to* them by grown-ups. The beautiful illustrations are done by JoAnn Dick, who illustrated "TA for Kids." Her art is unique, exciting and amusing. The 256 page text is an excellent teaching device and may be used with groups of children.

ORDER FORM — TEAR HERE

JALMAR Press, Inc., 391 Munroe Street, Sacramento, California 95825 — Telephone (916) 481-1134
Distributed to the trade by Price/Stern/Sloan Publishers, Inc., 410 N. La Cienega Boulevard,
Los Angeles, California 90048

Please send me the items indicated below:

_____ "TA for Tots (and other Prinzes)" paperback - $5.95 per copy, plus $.60 for postage and handling.

_____ "TA for Tots (and other Prinzes)" hardback (Buckram bound) $11.95 plus $.75 postage and handling.

_____ "Today I'm Okay" poster (see page 232) 18 x 11 - $2.00 each plus $.50 postage and handling.

NAME: _____

STREET: _____

CITY: _____

STATE _____ ZIP: _____

Enclosed is my check for _____
Prices subject to change without notice.

TOT-PAC

"TA for Tots (and other Prinzes)" is now available in an audio-visual program called "TOT-PAC"! All 34 characters in "Tots" are brought to life with individual voices, sound effects and musical scoring. Narration is by Dick Hardaway.

TOT-PAC is designed for use in classrooms, church schools, scouts and other youth groups. The 92 page leader's manual includes a complete storyboard, group discussion items, role plays, art projects and directions on presenting the program.

A record or cassette may be purchased separately for home or other use.

TOT-PAC includes:

*Set of 5 filmstrips** (avg. 42 frames each)
*Set of 5 cassettes or
*Set of 2 - 33-1/3 RPM records
*One copy *TA for TOTS (and other Prinzes)*
*92 page Leader's Manual
*Set of 8 *TA for Tots* character posters
*"The OKAY Society of the World Poster"
*Warm Fuzzies and Cold Pricklies

**Set of slides available at additional cost.

Also available separately:
    *55 minute cassette tape
    *2 - 33-1/3 RPM records

ORDER FORM — TEAR HERE

TOT-PAC, 391 Munroe Street, Sacramento, California 95825 — Telephone (916) 481-1134

Please send me the items indicated below:

_____ TOT-PAC - $85.00, plus $2.50 postage and handling.
_____ TOT-PAC with slides instead of filmstrip - $115.00, plus $2.50 postage and handling.
_____ 2 - 33-1/3 RPM records - $7.95, plus $.55 postage and handling
_____ 55 min. cassette tape - $6.95, plus $.45 postage and handling.
_____ Warm Fuzzies and Cold Pricklies $.25 each (minimum order 50), plus $.50 postage and handling.
_____ TA For Tots (and other Prinzes) $5.95 plus $.60 postage and handling.

NAME: _____

STREET: _____

CITY: _____

STATE: _____ ZIP: _____

California residents add 6% sales tax.
Prices subject to change without notice.